G000096463

This Head Teacher Appreciation Journal Belongs To:

Printed by Amazon Italia Logistica S.r.l.
Torrazza Piemonte (TO), Italy

11397411R00071